Key Stage 2

Forces and Electricity

Penny Johnson

Name ______________________________

Schofield&Sims

Introduction

Forces are around you all the time, whether you are moving or still. You use forces when you pick up a pencil from the floor, push open a door, or run across the playground. Electricity powers TVs, torches and other electrical items that you use in your home and at school. Electricity is very useful, but you need to know how to use it safely.

In this book you will find out about different kinds of force and what they do. You will also learn about electrical components and circuits.

How to use this book

Before you start using this book, write your name in the name box on the first page. Then decide how to begin. If you want a complete course on forces and electricity, you should work right through the book from beginning to end.

Another way to use the book is to dip into it when you want to find out about a particular topic. The Contents page or the index at the back of the book will help you to find the pages you need. Whichever way you choose, don't try to do too much at once – it's better to work through the book in short bursts.

When you have found the topic you want to study, look out for these icons, which mark different parts of the text.

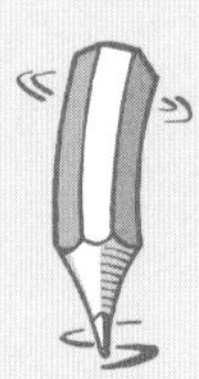

Activities

These are the activities that you should complete. You write your answers in the spaces. After you have worked through all the activities on the page, turn to pages 31 to 35 to check your answers. When you are sure that you understand the topic, put a tick in the box beside it on the Contents page.

Explanation

This text explains the topic and gives examples. Read it before you start the activities. Any words shown like **this** appear in the combined index and glossary. Look at page 36 to see what these words mean.

Information

This text gives you useful background information about the subject. Surprise your friends with some fascinating facts!

Contents

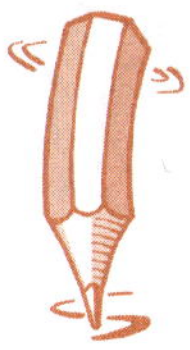

Tick the box when you have worked through the topic.

Magnets

Forces can:

- make objects start or stop moving
- make moving objects speed up or slow down
- make moving objects change direction
- change the shape of things.

A **magnet** can **attract** (pull) things made of **iron**. The pull of a magnet is a force.

Iron is a **magnetic material** because it can be picked up by a magnet. Steel is also a magnetic material, because it is mainly made of iron. Most other metals are **not** magnetic materials.

Did you know...?

Food cans are made from steel. Drinks cans are made from aluminium, which is not a magnetic material. You can use a magnet to sort out the different types of can for recycling.

1. Tick the boxes to show which things can be picked up with a magnet.

drinks can ☐

food can ☐

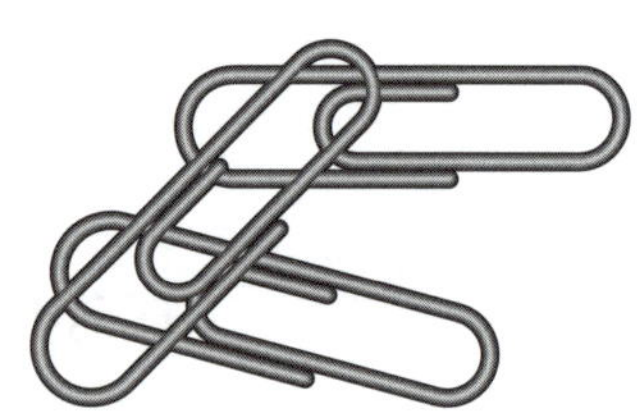
steel paper clips ☐

crisp packet ☐

iron nails ☐

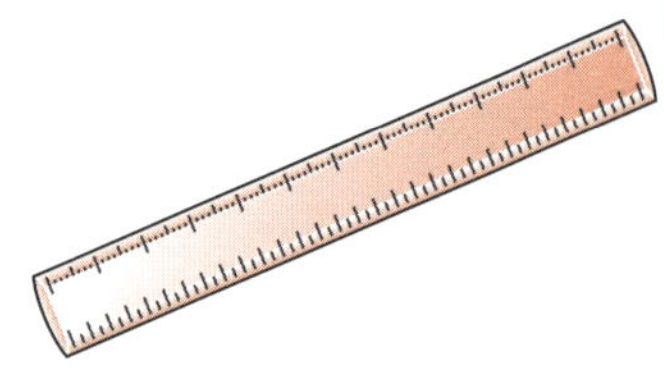
plastic ruler ☐

2. You can buy magnetic letters to stick to fridge doors.

a) What do you think the fridge door is made of? ____________

b) Why do you think this? ______________________________

____

Magnets

The two ends of a magnet are called North and South, because if you hang a magnet from a piece of string it will swing round until the North end is pointing north. The two ends are often painted in different colours.

Magnets can attract (pull) or **repel** (push) each other, depending on how they are arranged. You can use arrows to show the direction of the forces on the magnets.

These magnets will attract each other.

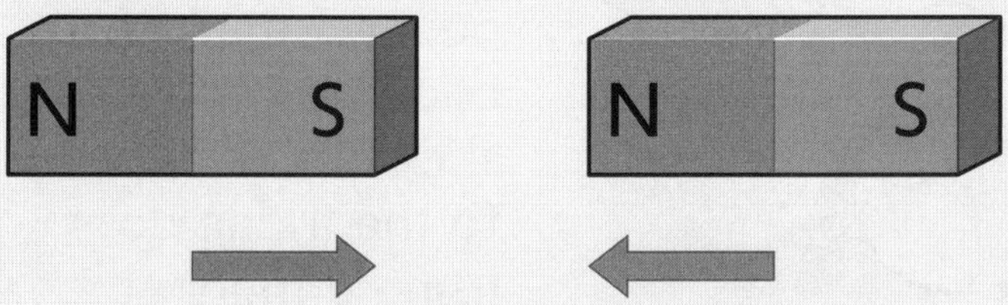

These magnets will repel each other.

Two magnets will repel each other if you hold similar ends together. They will attract each other if you hold opposite ends together.

3. Draw arrows under these magnets to show whether they will attract or repel each other.

a)

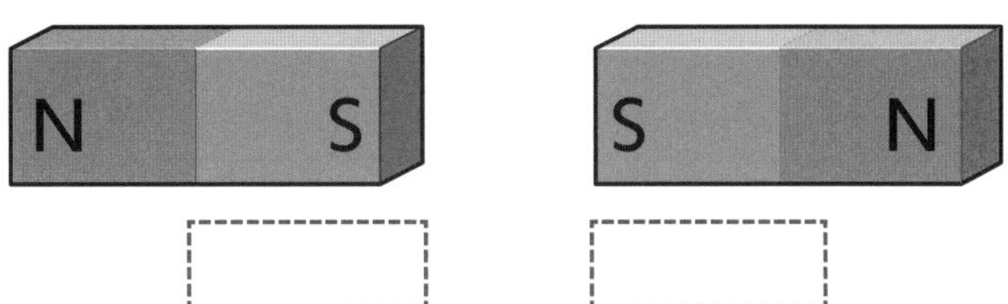

b)

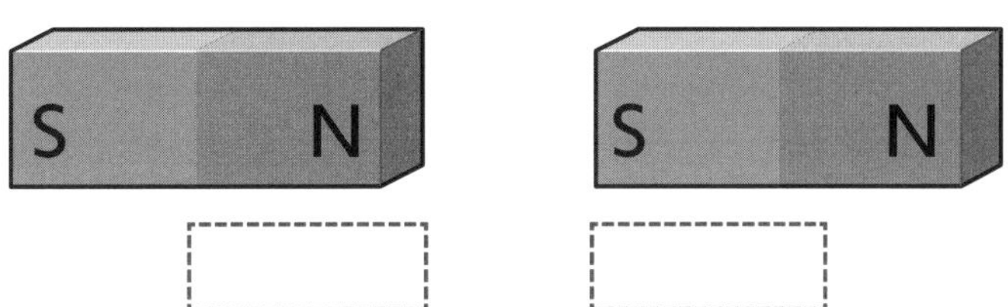

c)

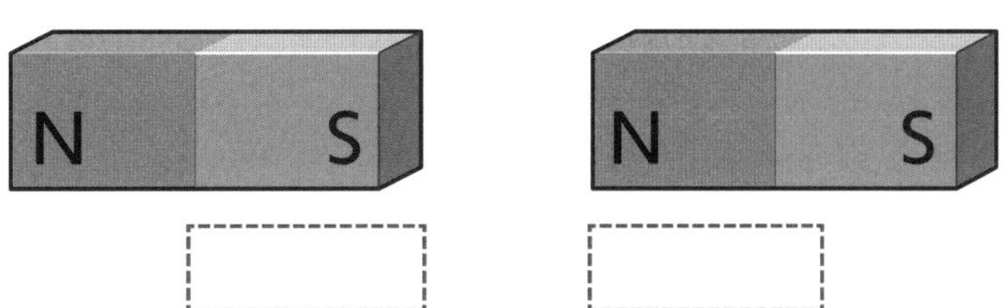

d)

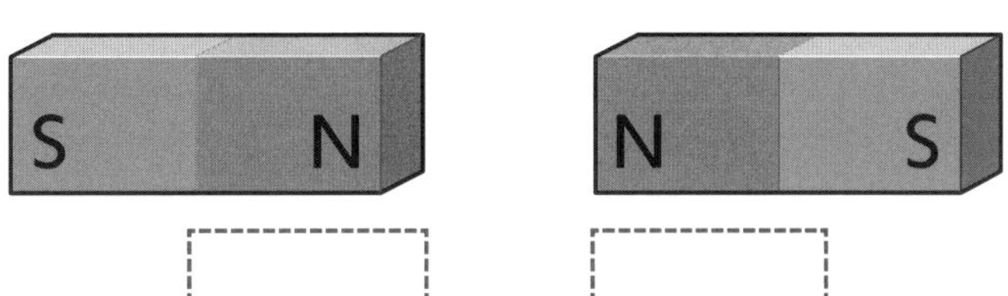

Testing magnets

Science is about **investigating** questions. A good scientific question is one that you can test. These are all good scientific questions about how a **magnet** works.

> Are big magnets stronger than small ones?

> Which materials will magnetism work through?

> How far away will a magnet attract things?

When you do an investigation, you might have an idea about what you will find. This is a **prediction**. You should always give a reason for your prediction.

Asha

> I think magnets will work through paper. I think this because I can stick bits of paper to the fridge door using a magnet.

1. Write a prediction for the first scientific question about magnets: 'Are big magnets stronger than smaller ones?' (It does not matter whether or not your prediction is correct.)

____

____

Asha tested her prediction by trying to pick up a paper clip with different materials under the magnet. She used the same magnet and paper clip each time, and she kept the same thickness of material. The only thing she changed was the kind of material.

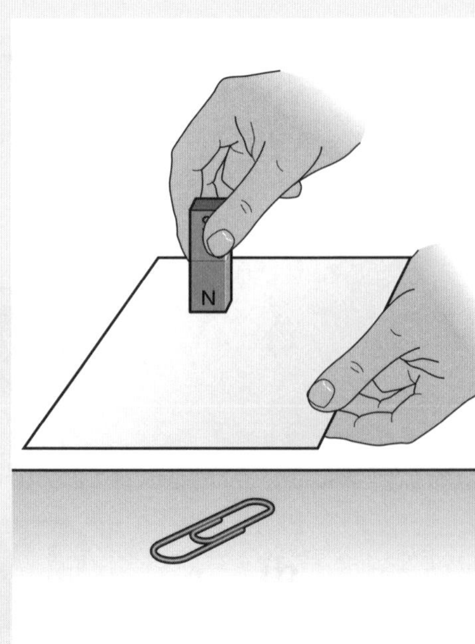

Asha's investigation was a **fair test** because she only changed one thing. If she had used a different magnet as well as a different material, she would not know if her result was because of the magnet or because of the material.

The table at the top of page 7 shows Asha's results.

Testing magnets

A **conclusion** is what you have found out in an experiment. Here is Asha's conclusion.

Magnets do not work through **iron**, but they work through other materials.

Material	Paper clip picked up?
paper	Yes
cotton fabric	Yes
iron	No
aluminium	Yes
plastic	Yes

2. What did Asha keep the same to make her test fair? ______________________

____

____

3. Was Asha's prediction correct? ____________

Ben tested different magnets to see which one was strongest. The bar chart shows his results.

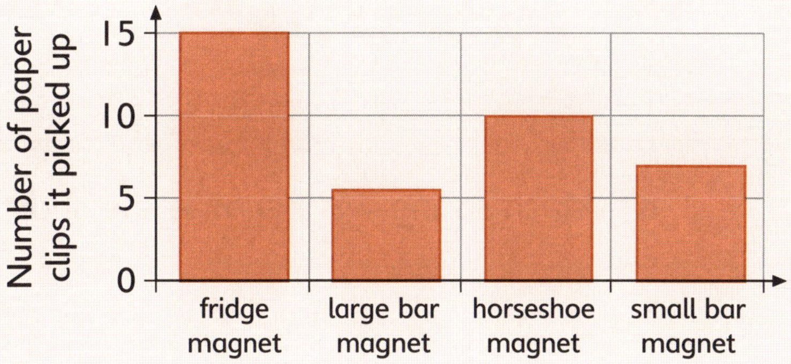

4. Which magnet picked up the most paper clips? ____________

5. Write a conclusion for Ben's experiment. ______________________

____

6. The paper clips that Ben used were a mixture of different sizes. Explain why Ben's experiment may not have been a fair test.

____

____

Springs

A **spring** is stretchy. You can pull springs to **stretch** them (make them longer). You can push springs to **compress** them (make them shorter).

When you pull on a spring you can feel it pulling back. The harder you pull on a spring, the more it stretches and the harder it pulls back.

Use big arrows to show large **forces**, and small arrows to show small forces.

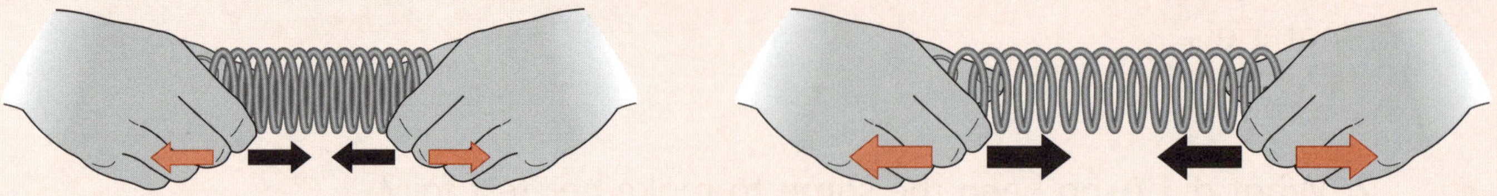

A similar thing happens when you push on springs. The harder you push, the shorter they get and the more they push back.

1. a) Which spring will stretch the most? ____________

b) Which spring will become the shortest? ____________

2. Draw force arrows on these springs to show how much each spring is pushing or pulling back.

a) **b)**

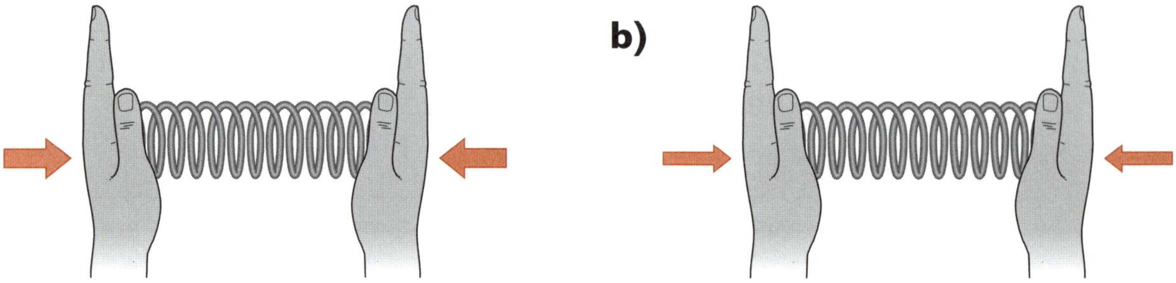

Springs

You can measure forces using a **forcemeter**. Forcemeters have springs inside them. The harder you pull on the spring, the more it stretches. You can read the size of the force on the **scale**.

Different forcemeters have different scales. You need to use the correct forcemeter for the size of the forces you are going to measure.

Forces are measured in units called **newtons**. You can write this as **N** for short.

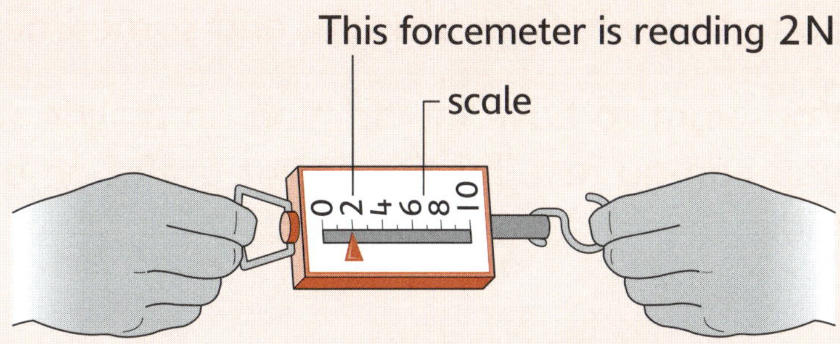

3. What forces are pulling on these forcemeters?

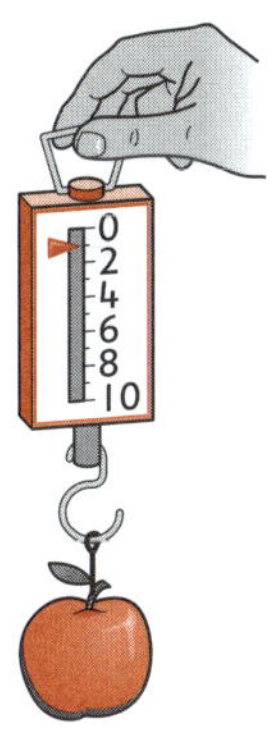

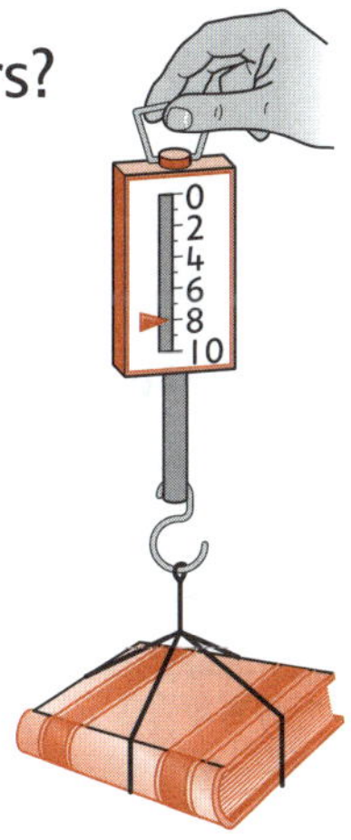

a) ______________

b) ______________

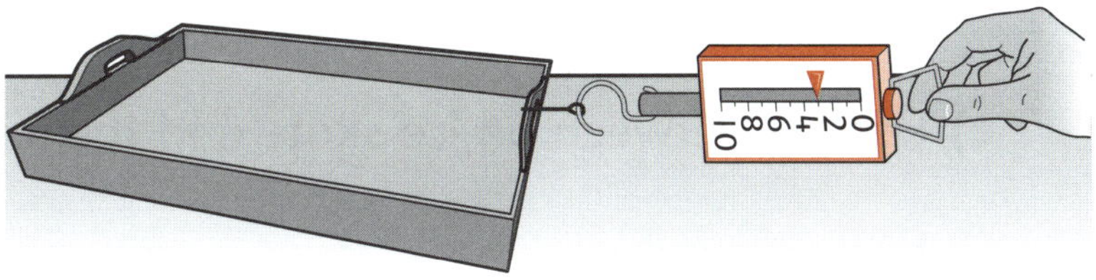

c) ______________

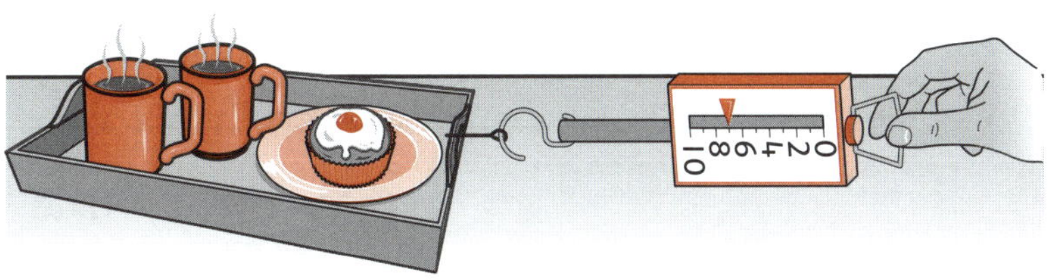

d) ______________

Did you know...

The units for force are named after Sir Isaac Newton, who worked out how forces can change the way things move. Sir Isaac Newton also made many other discoveries about light and **gravity**.

Friction

Friction is a force that slows down moving things. It can sometimes stop something starting to move. The more friction there is, the more things slow down.

Sometimes friction is useful and sometimes it is not useful.

You want to have low friction on a slide so you can go fast. Friction is not useful on a slide.

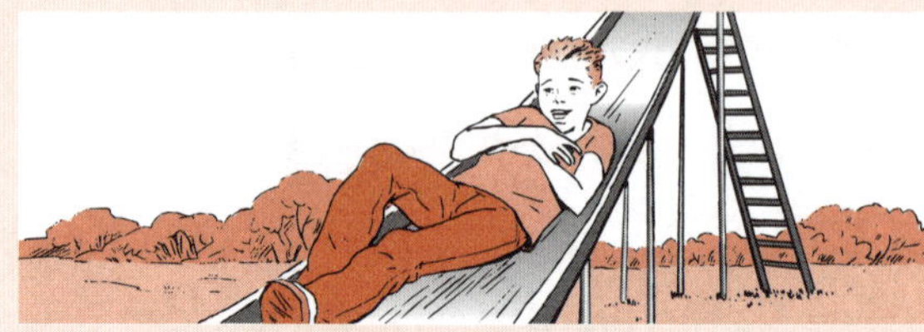

You need high friction between your shoes and the pavement to stop you slipping. Friction is useful when you are walking.

1. These are all places where you find friction. Say whether the friction is useful or not useful, and explain your answers.

a) Friction between your shoes and the floor is ______________________

because ______________________________________.

b) Friction between a car's tyres and the road is ______________________

because ______________________________________.

c) Friction between an ice skate and the ice is ______________________

because ______________________________________.

d) Friction between a bicycle wheel and the axle is ______________________

because ______________________________________.

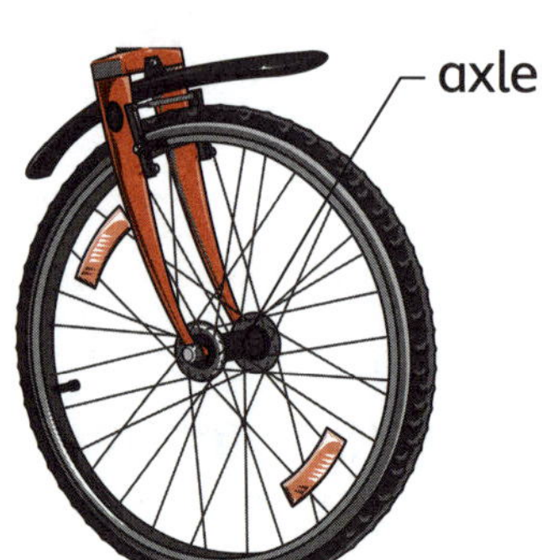

Friction

The amount of friction depends on the surfaces that are rubbing together. It is easy to get a grip on rough surfaces because they have high friction. Smooth surfaces are slippery because they have low friction. You can make a surface smoother by polishing it. The smoother the surface, the lower the friction.

Ice usually has a very smooth surface, so it is very slippery.

2. What kind of material should these things be made from? Write 'rough' or 'smooth' in the first space in each sentence, and then explain your answers.

a) A slide should be made from a __________ material because

____.

b) Roads should be made from a __________ material because

____.

3. Why do cars sometimes skid off the road in the winter?

____.

4. Mr Smith has polished half of the piece of wood. Carol and Danny are flicking dice using the same force.

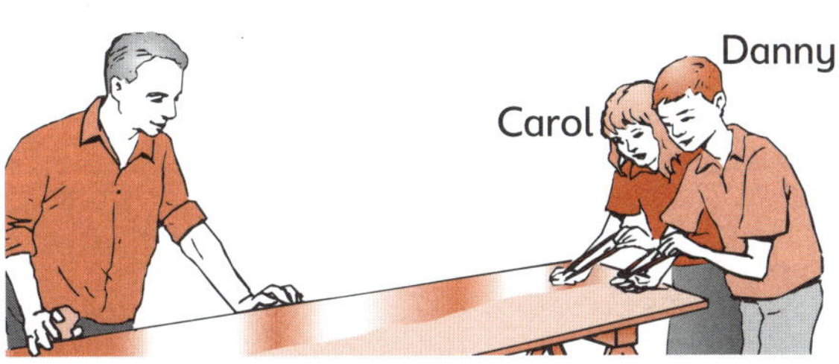

a) Whose dice will go the furthest? ____________________

b) Explain your answer. ____________________

____

____

Investigating friction

Ellie investigated different trainers to find out which ones have the best grip. She used a **forcemeter** to pull each trainer along a piece of wood. She wrote down the force needed to pull each one.

1. Ellie tested four different trainers. What must she have kept the same each time to make her test fair? (You may need to look back at pages 6 and 7 to remind yourself about fair tests.)

____

____

The table shows Ellie's results.

Trainer	Force needed to pull it (N)
A	4.0
B	2.0
C	3.5
D	5.0

You can show the results of some scientific investigations using a bar chart. This bar chart shows Ellie's results.

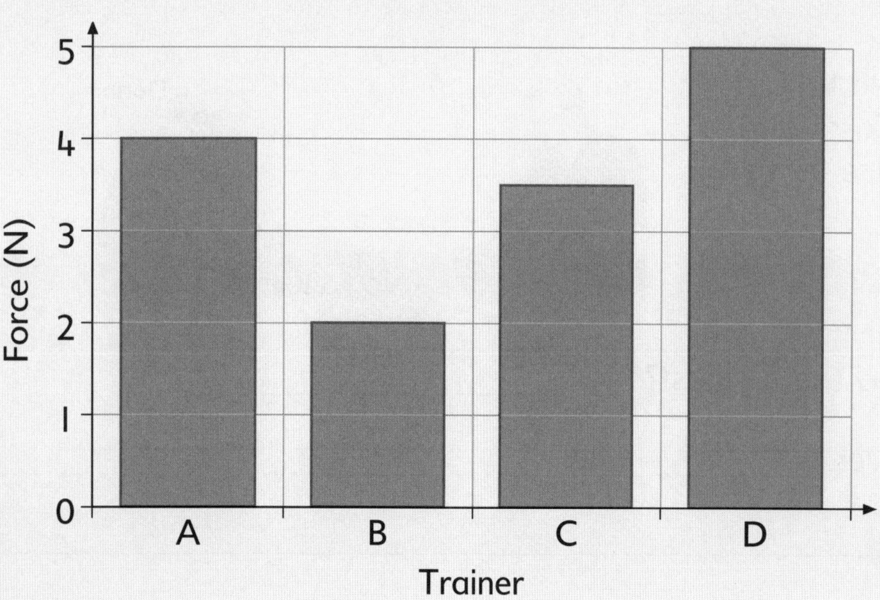

Investigating friction

2. a) Which trainer needed the most force to pull it? __________

b) Which trainer had the best grip? __________

c) Which trainer had the smallest force of friction between the trainer and the wood? __________

d) Which trainer had the worst grip? __________

The **conclusion** is what you have found out in an investigation. Your answers to question 2 tell you all you need to know to write a conclusion for Ellie's investigation.

3. Write a conclusion for Ellie's investigation.

____

____

When you have carried out an investigation, you also need to say how good you think your results were. This is called an **evaluation**. This is Ellie's evaluation.

> It was difficult to read the **forcemeter** while I was pulling the training shoes. My results might be more accurate if I repeated the tests. I think my investigation was good because I did a **fair test**.

4. Why did Ellie think she should have repeated the tests?

____

Water resistance

Water resistance is a kind of **friction**. It slows down things that are moving through water. Things with a smooth, pointed shape have the lowest water resistance.

Fish have smooth shapes to help them to move through the water. Their shape gives them a low water resistance so it is easy for them to swim fast.

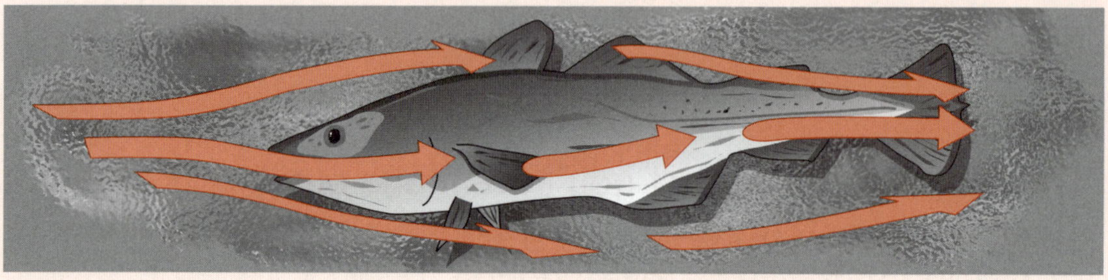

1. Why are boats usually pointed at the front?

____

2. Faruk drops two shapes into the swimming pool. They are both the same **weight**.

a) Which shape will reach the bottom of the pool first? ____________

b) Explain your answer.

____

____

c) Why is it important that both shapes are the same weight?

____

____

Air resistance

Air resistance is also a kind of friction. It slows down things that are moving through air. The amount of air resistance depends on the shape and the size of the object.

- The larger the object, the greater the air resistance.
- The smoother the shape of the object, the lower the air resistance.

Sometimes you can feel air resistance when you are not moving. The wind is moving air, so it can push against us.

1. a) Who will have lower air resistance, Ian or Jane? ____________

b) Explain your answer.

____

____

2. Sam and Pen are the same weight.

a) Who falls more slowly? ____________

b) Explain your answer. ____________

____

____

3. The graph shows Erik's results.

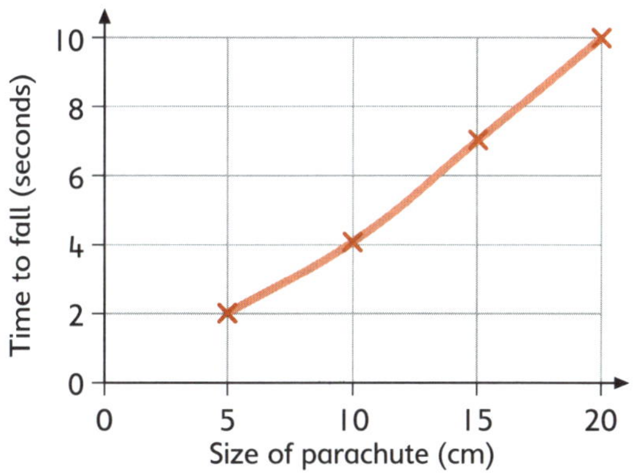

a) What was he **investigating**?

____

____

b) What does Erik's graph show? ____________________________

c) The bigger the parachute, the ____________ the air resistance and the ____________ it takes to fall.

Gravity and weight

You can measure pulling and pushing **forces** using a **forcemeter**. You can also use a forcemeter to find the **weight** of something. Weight is a force, so we measure weight in **newtons**.

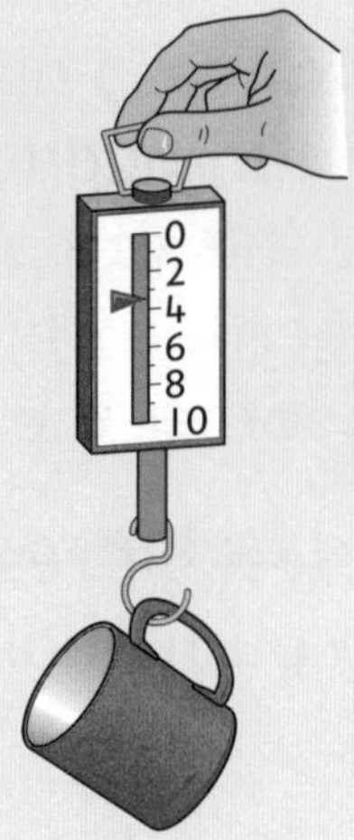

Gemma is measuring the weight of the mug.

Gravity is a force that pulls things towards each other. You are being pulled towards the Earth, and the Earth is also being pulled towards you!

The weight of an object is the size of the force of gravity pulling it towards the Earth.

Did you know...

The Moon has gravity, but it is not as strong as the Earth's gravity. If you went to the Moon your weight would only be one sixth of your weight on the Earth.

1. Fill in the missing words in these sentences.

A force called ______________________ pulls things towards the ______________________. Your ______________________ is the size of the ______________________ of gravity on you. The units for weight are ______________________.

2. An apple weighs 1 N on the Earth. How much would it weigh on the Moon? ____________

Balanced forces

Harry is holding a football. The weight of the ball is pulling downwards, so there has to be an upwards force from Harry's hand to stop the ball falling to the ground.

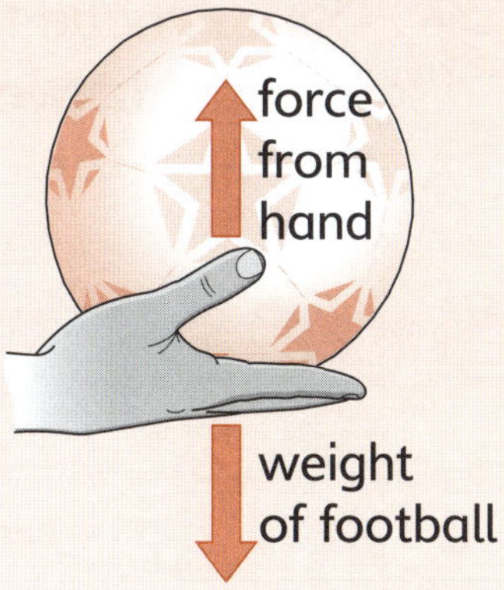

The two **forces** are the same size, but in opposite directions. These are **balanced forces**. All **stationary** (not moving) things have balanced forces on them.

1. Ian and John are not moving. Draw arrows to show the force each boy is putting on the rope. (Remember that the size of the arrow shows the size of the force.)

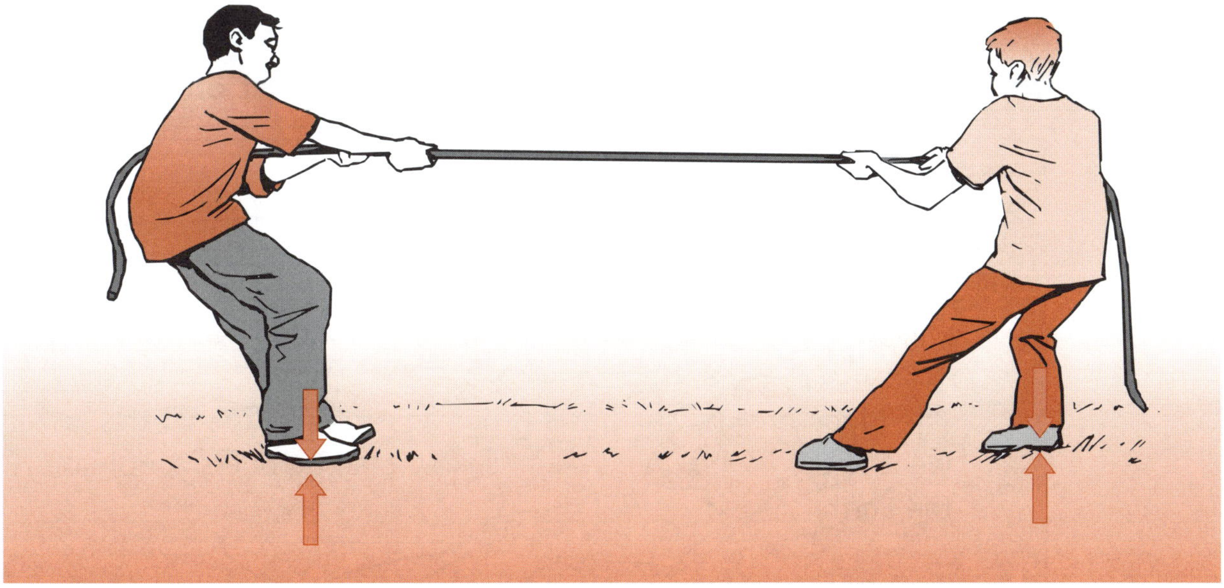

2. Draw arrows to show the missing forces in these diagrams.

a)

b)

Floating and upthrust

Things made from wood will **float** on water. When something is floating, its weight is balanced by a force called **upthrust**.

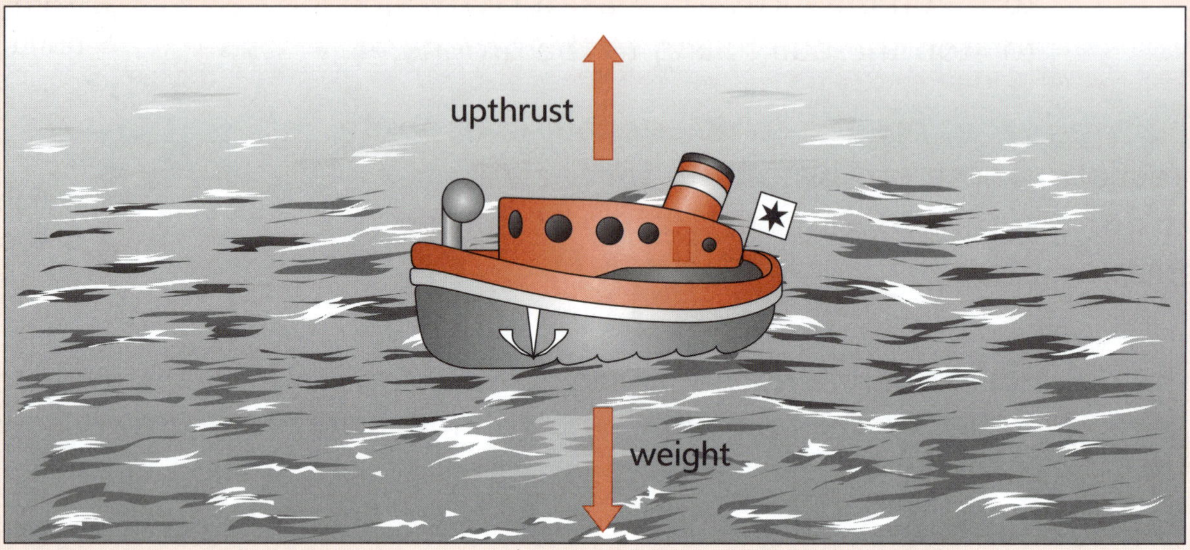

1. a) Jackie's **weight** is 150 N. What is the upthrust on her? ___________

b) Jackie's mum weighs 700 N. What is the upthrust on Jackie's mum?

____

Did you know...?

A lump of metal will sink, because there is not enough upthrust to balance its weight. Ships made from metal can float because they have large air spaces inside them.

Floating and upthrust

A stone will sink, not float. This is because the upthrust is not big enough to balance its weight. There **is** still upthrust on the stone.

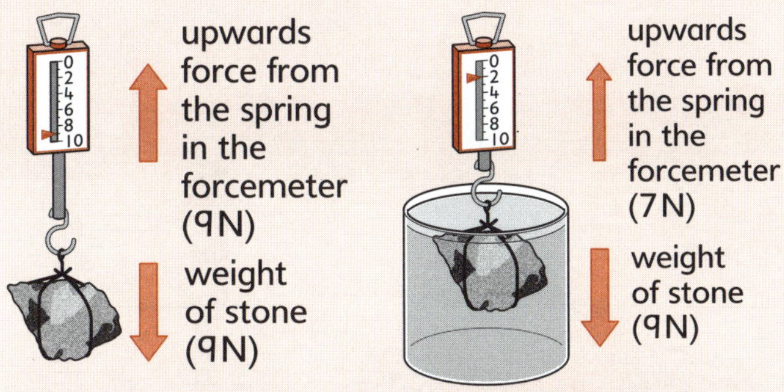

You can measure the upthrust using a **forcemeter**. The stone in the drawings on the left weighs 9 N, but it only seems to weigh 2 N when it is in water, because the upthrust balances some of its weight.

You can do the same thing with something that floats, such as a ball. There is no force from the forcemeter because the upthrust completely balances the weight.

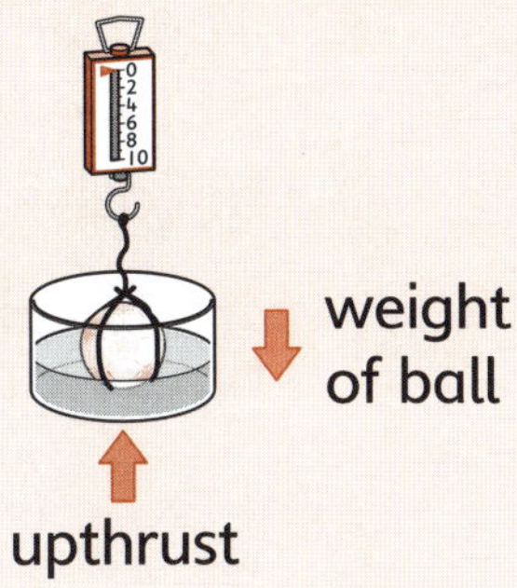

2. When you float in a swimming pool, what is the name of the force that is balancing your weight? ____________

3. Look at the drawings of the stone.

a) How much does the stone weigh? ____________

b) What is the upthrust on the stone when it is in water? ____________

c) How much force from the forcemeter is needed to balance the weight of the stone when it is in water? ____________

d) Explain why your answers to parts **a)** and **c)** are different.

____

____

4. Kai weighed a bar of soap in air and in water. Draw arrows on the pictures to show all the **forces**. Label your arrows. One arrow has been drawn for you.

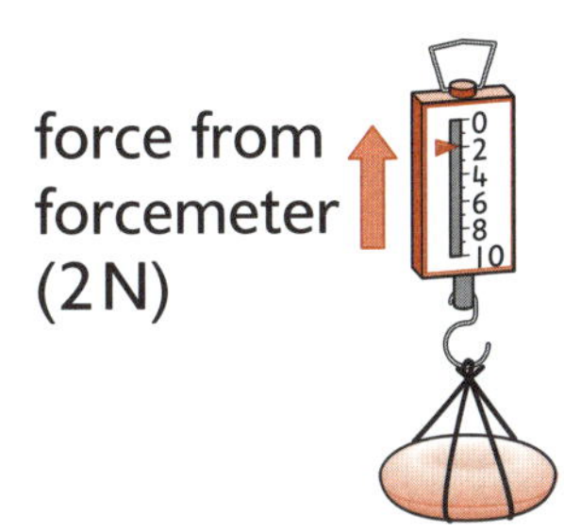

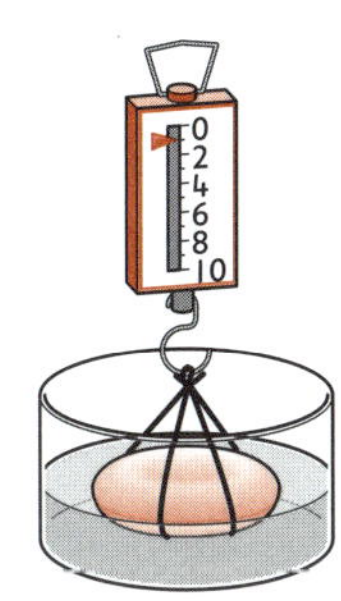

Unbalanced forces

The forces on a **stationary** object are **balanced forces**. If there are **unbalanced forces** on something, it can:

- start or stop moving
- speed up or slow down
- change the direction it is moving.

The car shown in the picture will speed up because the forwards force is bigger than the backwards force.

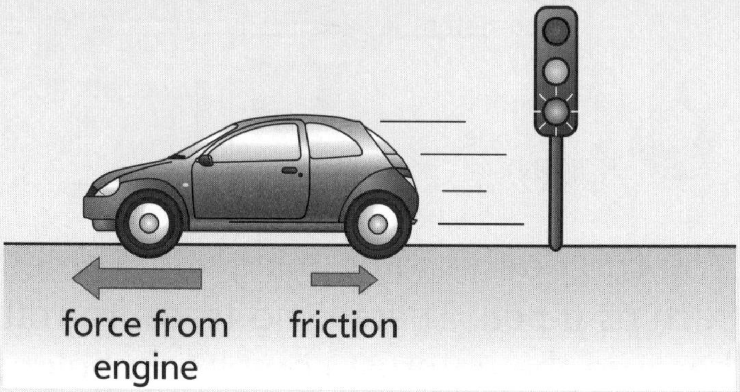

Here, the car will slow down because the backwards force is bigger than the forwards force.

The ball changes direction because of the force from the bat.

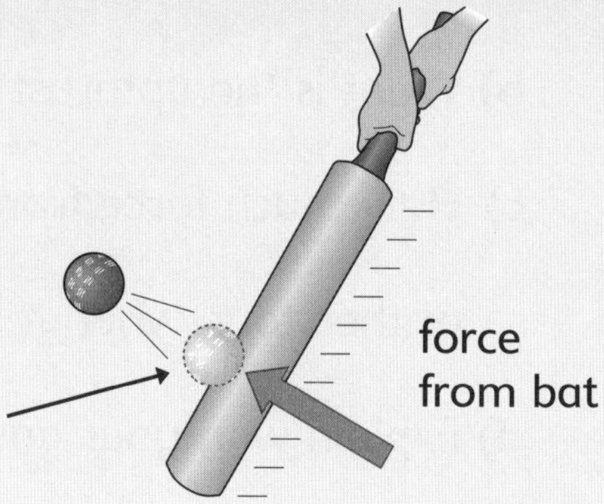

Leah will fall faster and faster until she hits the water.

Unbalanced forces

1. What will happen to the speed of these cars?

a) ______________________ **b)** ______________________

2. Mark is playing on a slide.

a) Why does Mark speed up as he starts to go down the slide?

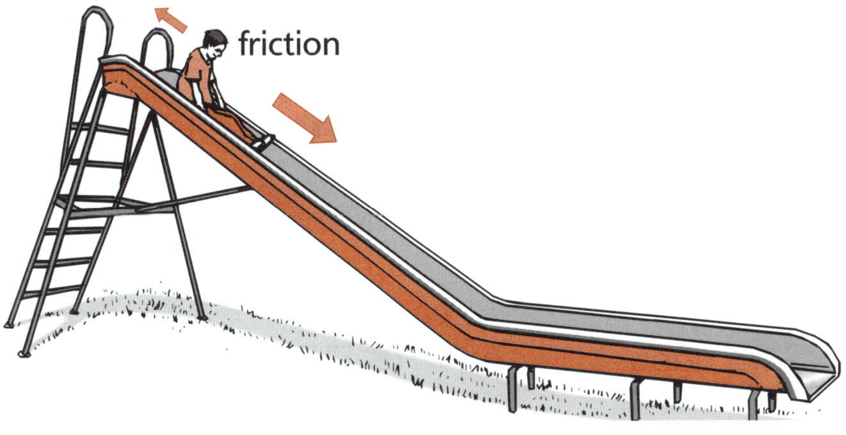

____

b) Why does Mark slow down at the end of the slide?

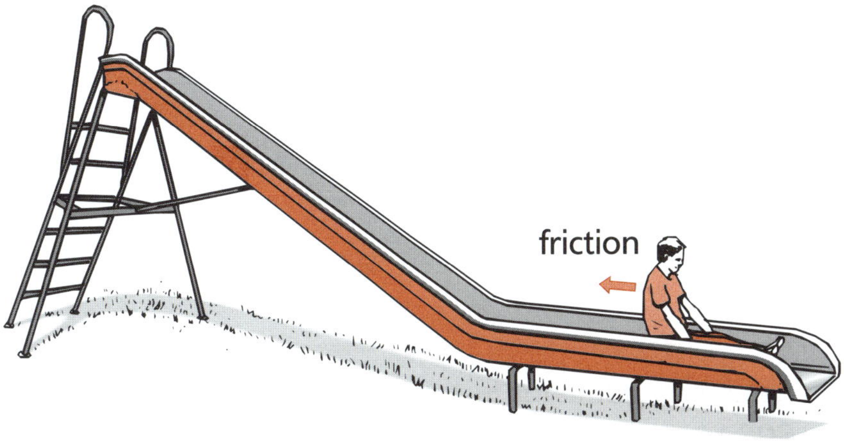

____

Electrical circuits

The drawing shows an **electrical circuit**. Each different thing in the circuit is called a **component**. Each component does a different job.

The **battery** provides the electricity.

The wires join all the parts of the circuit together.

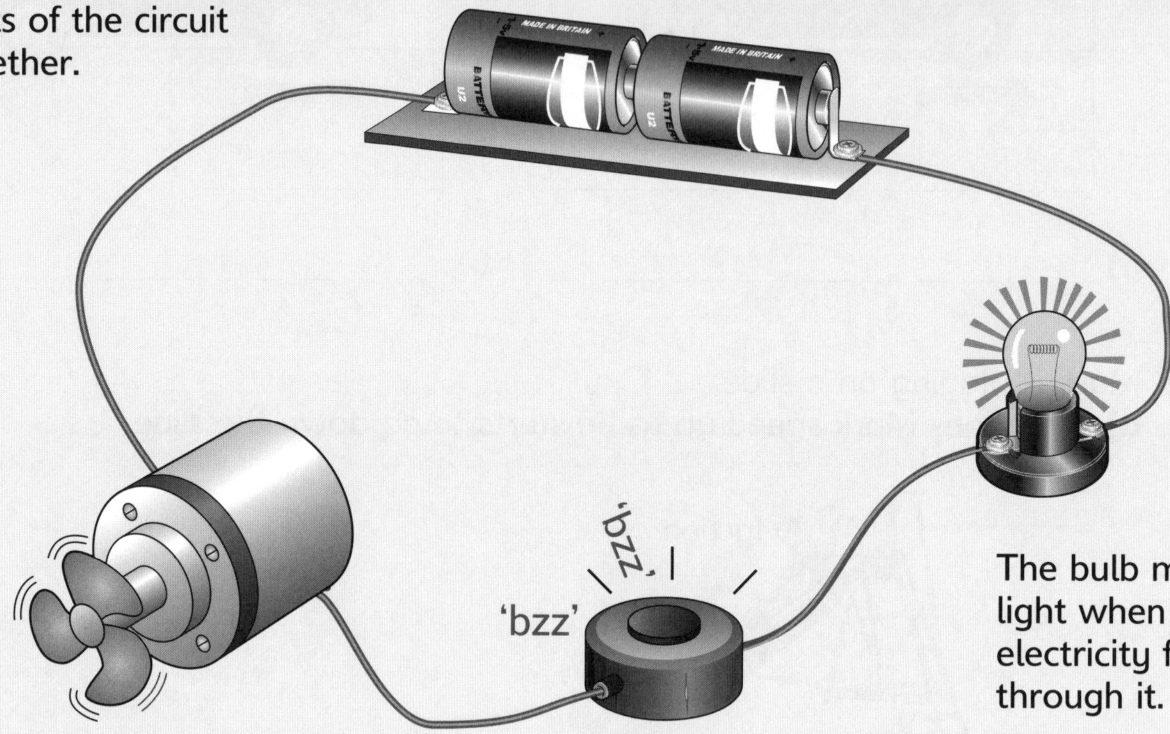

The bulb makes light when electricity flows through it.

The motor turns when electricity flows through it.

The buzzer makes a noise when electricity flows through it.

1. What do these components do?

a) battery ______________________________

b) motor ______________________________

c) wires ______________________________

Did you know...

The correct name for just one battery is **cell**. The first cell was built in 1800 by an Italian scientist called Alessandro Volta.

Electrical circuits

The parts of the circuit have to be joined in a complete loop for it to work. If there is a gap in the circuit, it will not work.

Switches work by making or closing a gap in the circuit. The bulb in this circuit is not lit because there is a gap in the circuit.

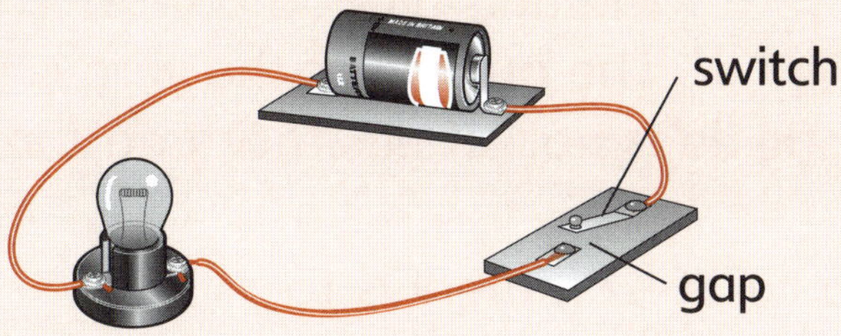

If you press the switch, it closes the gap and joins up the wires. Electricity can flow around the circuit and the bulb lights up.

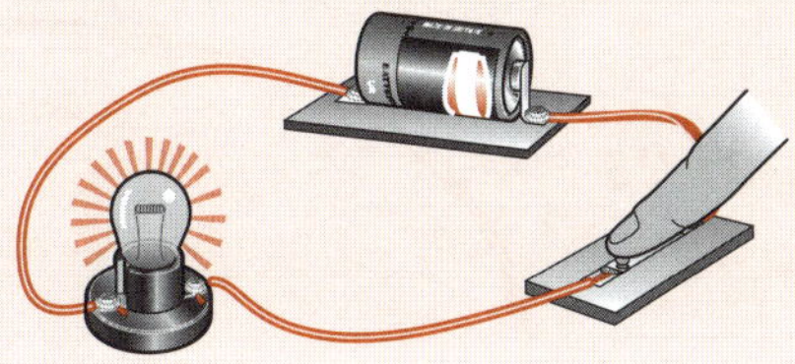

2. What is wrong with these circuits?

a) ______________________________

____

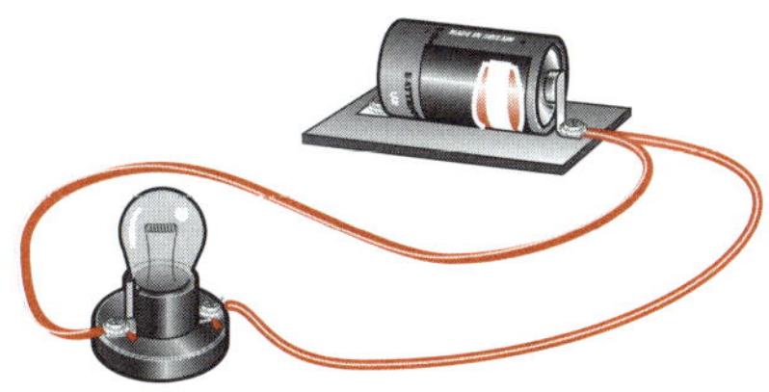

b) ______________________________

____

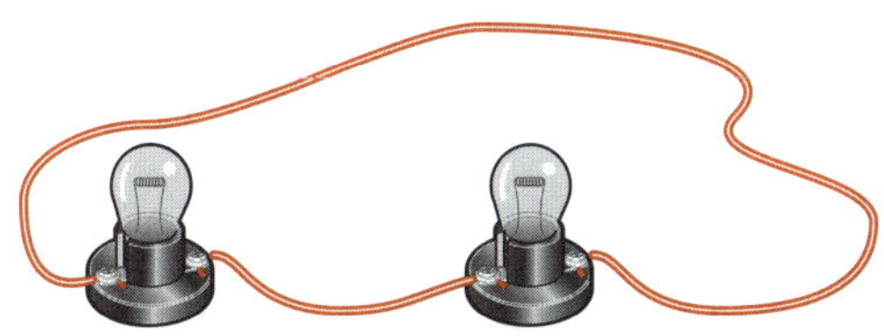

c) ______________________________

____

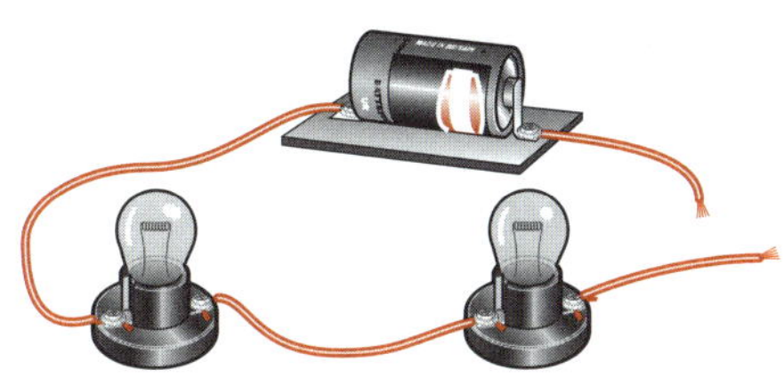

3. a) How can you make the bulb light up in this circuit?

____

____

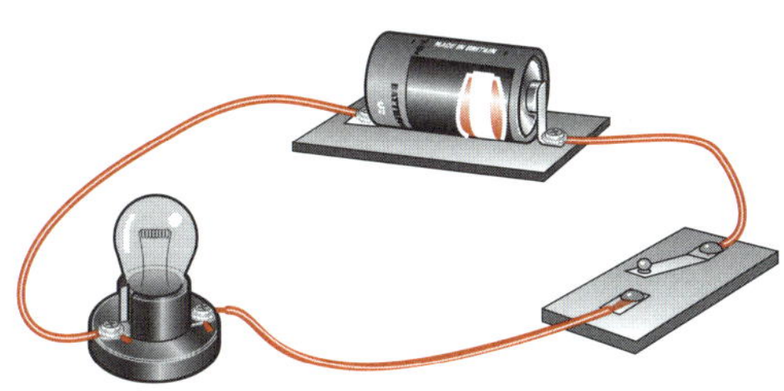

b) Explain why doing this will make the bulb light up. ______________________________

____

____

Conductors and insulators

The wires in a circuit are made from metal. Metal allows electricity to flow through it. Metal is a good **conductor** of electricity. The outside of the wire is covered in plastic. Plastic does not let electricity go through it. Plastic is an **insulator**.

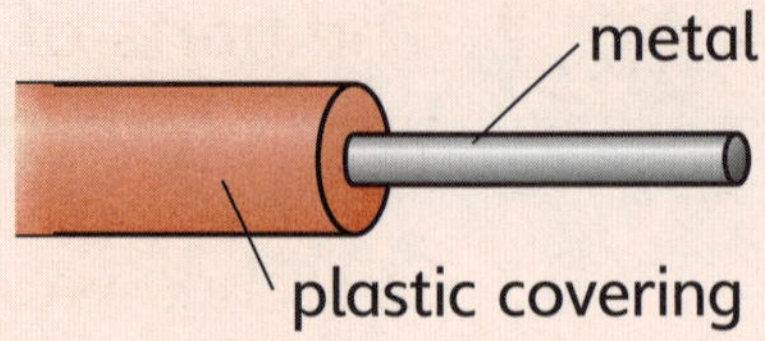

You can test materials to find out which ones are conductors and which ones are insulators.

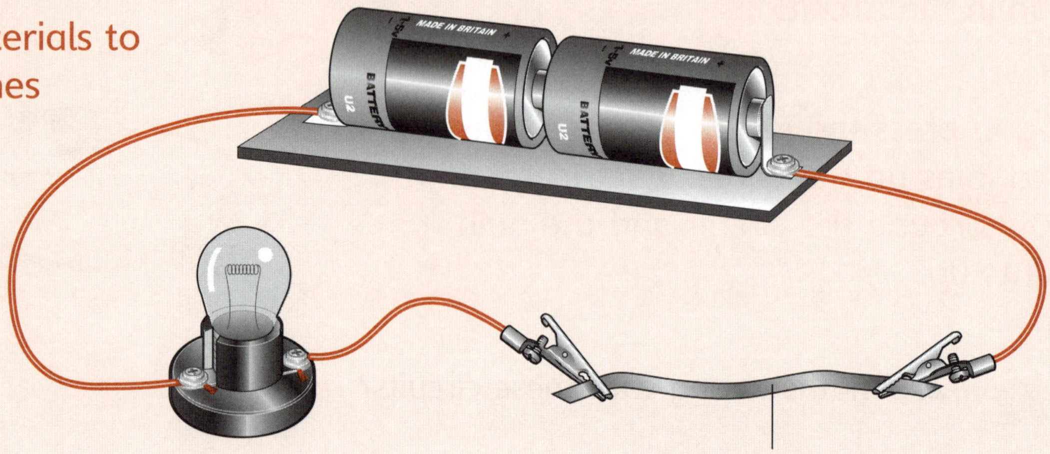

1. Why are wires made from metal?

____

2. Nat tests some different materials. He uses the circuit shown in the drawing above.

a) Will the bulb light up when he tests a coin? ____________

b) Why will this happen? ____________________________

3. The bulb does not light up when he tests wood, plastic and glass. Complete this table to show the results of Nat's investigation.

Material	Does the bulb light?	Conductor or insulator?
wood	✗	insulator
coin		
plastic ruler		
metal scissors		
drinking glass		

Staying safe

The electricity from a **cell** is not very powerful. So the cells you use at school, or in things like torches or MP3 players, are very safe.

Many machines need **mains electricity**. This is much more powerful than the electricity from a cell, and it can hurt you or even kill you if it flows through you.

You can use electricity safely by following some simple rules.

Safety with electricity

- Never poke things into sockets or take electrical machines apart.
- Never touch the bare metal parts of plugs.
- Never touch switches with wet hands, and keep electrical things away from water.
- Don't use electrical machines if they have damaged wires.

1. Why is it safer to use batteries than mains electricity?

____

2. Write down four dangerous things that are happening in this picture.

- ____
- ____
- ____
- ____

Drawing circuits

You can use **symbols** to draw an **electrical circuit**. It is easier to draw a symbol to represent a **component** than it is to draw the actual component.

We always use the same symbol for each component, so that everyone can understand. We draw straight lines for wires so that the **circuit diagram** looks neat and tidy.

The symbols you need to know are shown in the table below.

Name	**Picture**	**Symbol**
cell	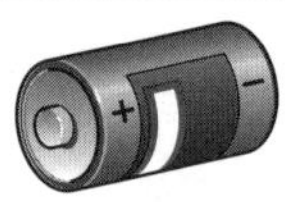	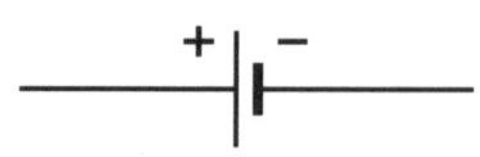
wire		
battery	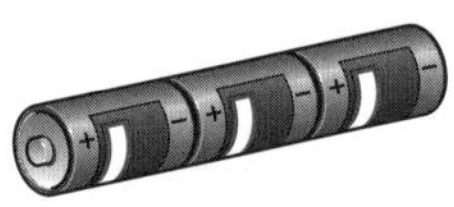	
open switch		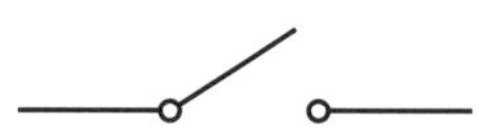
closed switch		
bulb		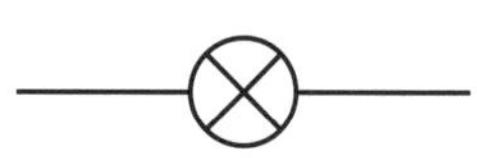
motor	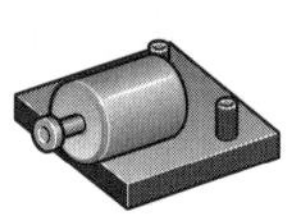	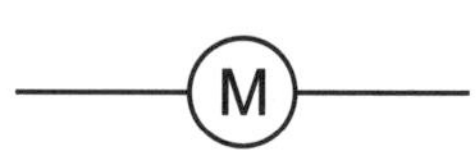
buzzer		

Did you know...?

A **battery** is two or more cells used together.

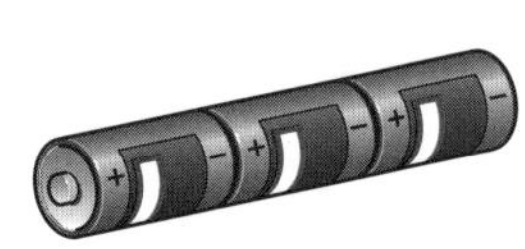

Drawing circuits

This is a picture of a circuit ...

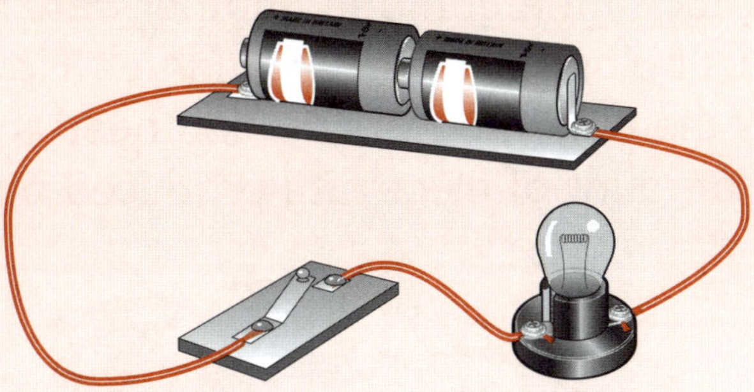

... and this is the circuit diagram.

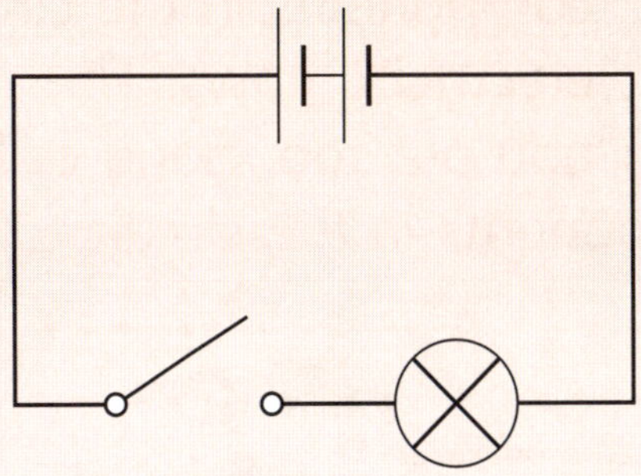

1. Draw the symbols for:

a) a bulb

b) a cell

c) an open switch

2. Draw circuit diagrams for these circuits. The first one has been started for you.

a)

b)

c)

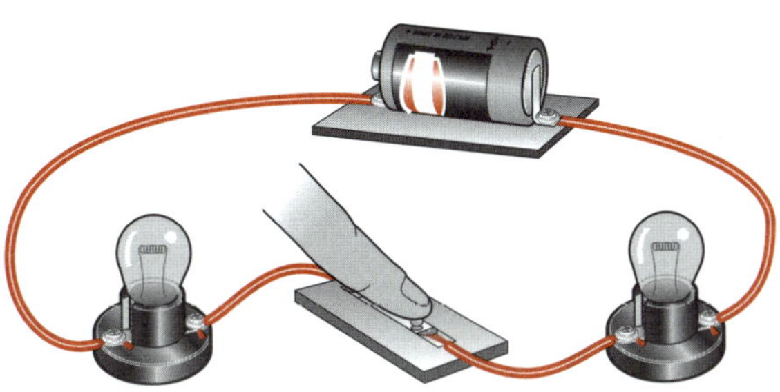

Changing components

The amount of electricity flowing in a circuit depends on the components in the circuit. Each time you add another **cell**, more electricity flows. This makes bulbs in the circuit brighter. However, if you put too many cells in, the bulb may break. You need to match the components in the circuit to the amount of electricity produced by the cells.

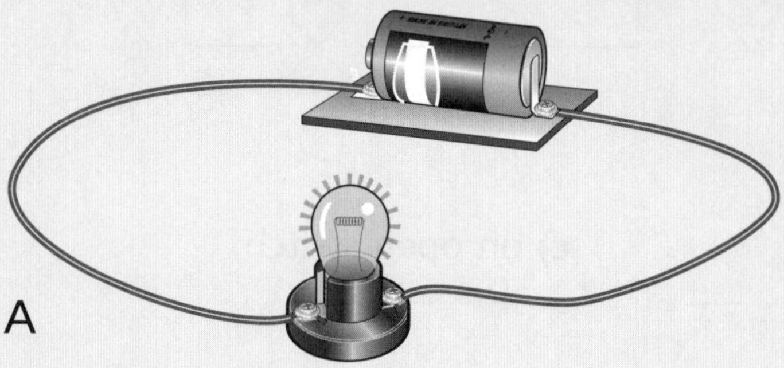

A

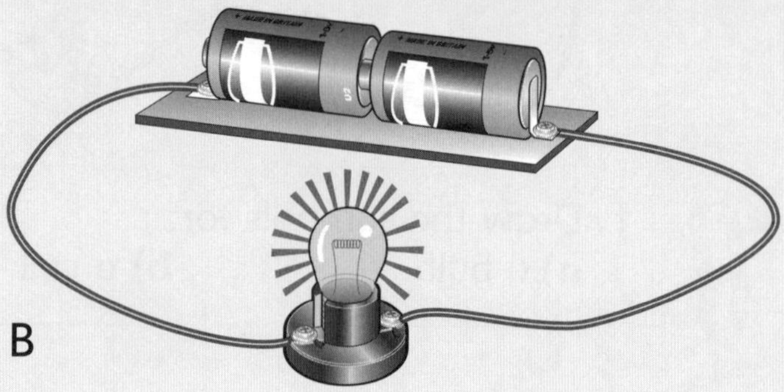

B

If you add more bulbs, the electricity is shared between the bulbs so they are not as bright.

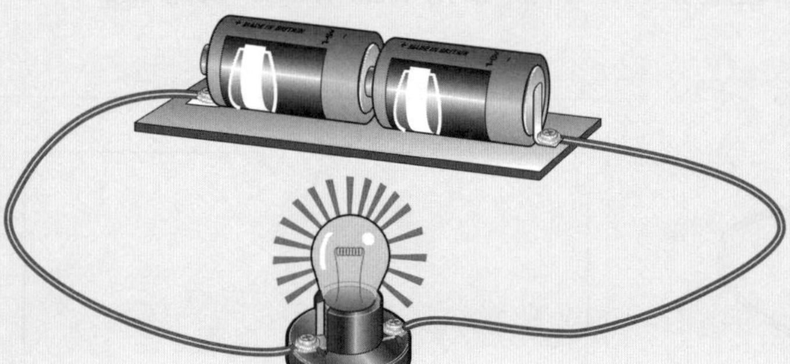

C

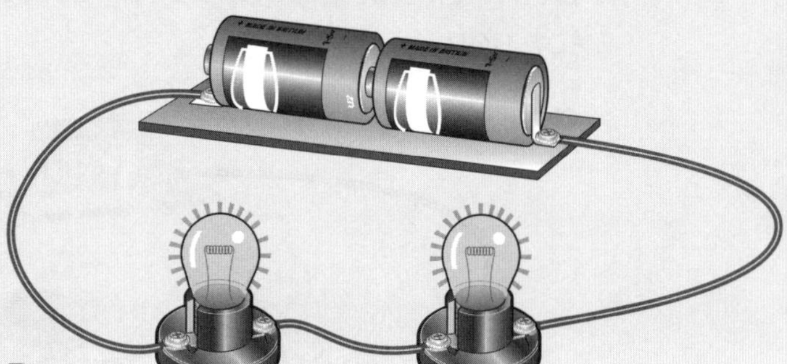

D

1. How can you tell that more electricity is flowing in circuit B than in circuit A?

____

2. How could you make the bulb in circuit B even brighter?

____

3. How could you make the bulbs in circuit D dimmer? (There are two ways.)

- ______________________________________
- ______________________________________

Changing components

You can also change the amount of electricity in a circuit by making it more difficult for electricity to flow.

It is harder for electricity to flow through a thin wire than through a thick one. If you put a piece of thin wire in a circuit, less electricity will flow in the circuit.

Tom wanted to find out if the length of the wire changes the amount of electricity flowing in the circuit. The graph shows his results.

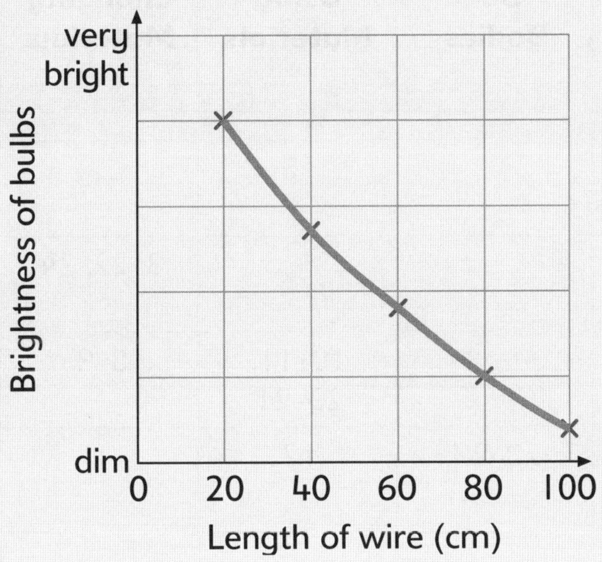

4. Look at the graph. Fill in the gaps using the words from the brackets.

The bulb was brightest when Tom had the ______________________ (longest/shortest) wire in his circuit. This means that it is easier for electricity to flow through a ___________ (long/short) wire. The shorter the wire, the ______________________ (greater/smaller) the amount of electricity that can flow.

5. Tick the box next to the wire that it will be the hardest for electricity to flow through.

- ☐ a short, thin wire
- ☐ a short, thick wire
- ☐ a long, thin wire
- ☐ a long, thick wire

Scientific investigation

In this book you have found out about different kinds of forces, and about electrical circuits. You have also learnt how to investigate some scientific questions. Good scientists need many different skills in order to investigate things. You can learn some of the other skills you need in the other **Understanding Science** books. The table below shows you the skills you need, and which books help to teach you these skills or give you practice in using them.

Skill	**Book pages**					
	Animals and Plants	**Our Bodies**	**Using Materials**	**Changing Materials**	**Forces and Electricity**	**Light, Sound and Space**
Planning an investigation						
Asking a scientific question			10		6	
Knowing what factors are	6–7			8, 22, 24		6–7
Planning a fair test	6–7		10–11, 20–21	8–9	6–7, 12	6–7, 16
Predicting what you think you will find out		28–29	17		6–7	16
Recording and presenting your evidence						
Making tally charts		27				
Drawing pictograms		8				
Drawing bar charts		8, 27	12–13, 20	22–23, 24–25		
Drawing line graphs		28–29		10, 22–23, 24–25		6–7
Considering your evidence and evaluating it						
Writing a conclusion	6–7	9	12–13, 20	9, 10, 25	7, 13	
Evaluating your investigation	6–7	9, 26	13	9, 10	13	17

Answers

Pages 4 and 5

1. You should have put a tick next to the food can, the steel paper clips and the iron nails.

2. **a)** iron (or steel)
b) Iron (or steel) is a magnetic material. The letters would not stick to the door if it was not a magnetic material.

3.

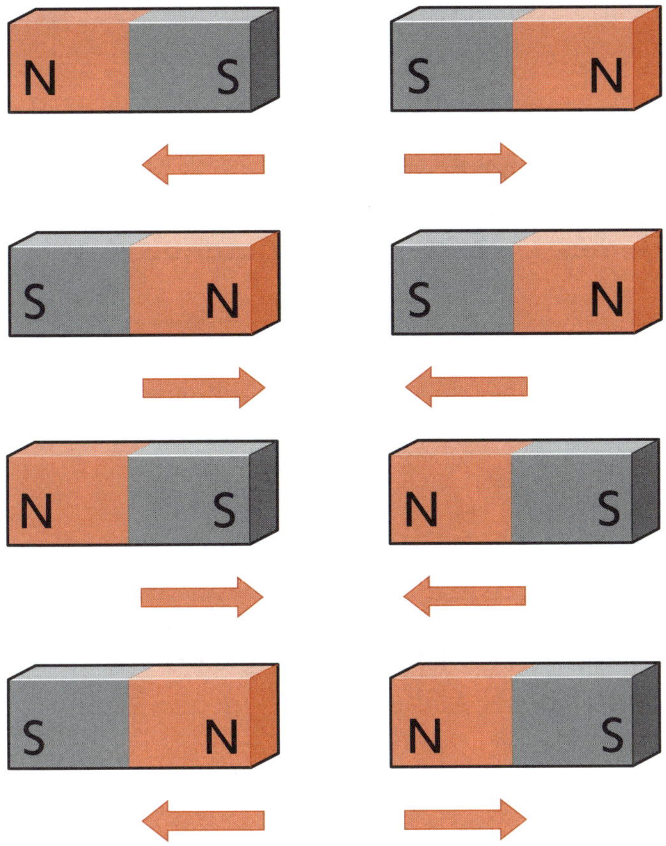

Pages 6 and 7

1. You could have written 'Big magnets are stronger than small ones' **or** 'The size of the magnet does not tell you its strength.'

2. The magnet and the paper clip, and the same thickness of material.

3. yes

4. the fridge magnet

5. The fridge magnet was the strongest, because it picked up the most paper clips.

6. Your explanation could be something like this: 'If two magnets picked up different numbers of paper clips, you would not know if it was because one was stronger than the other, or was picking up smaller paper clips'.

Pages 8 and 9

1. **a)** B
b) A

Answers

2. a)

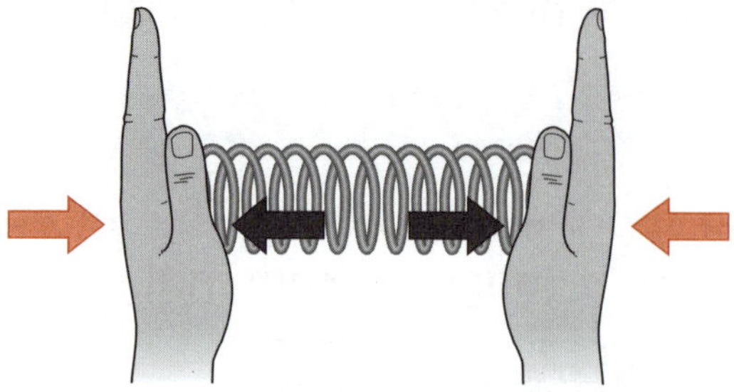

b)

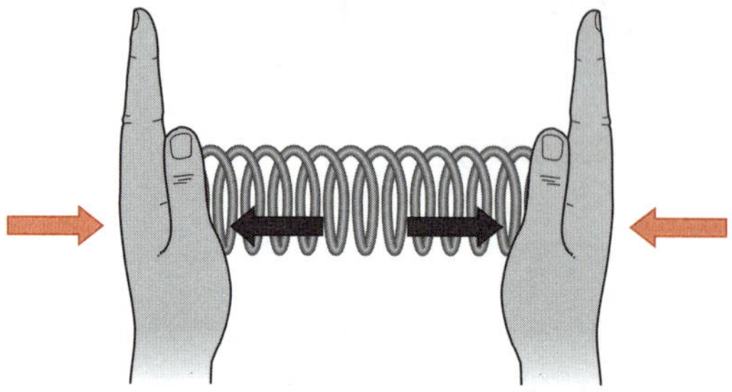

3. a) 1 N
b) 8 N
c) 3 N
d) 7 N

Pages 10 and 11

1. These are some suggested answers. Make sure your explanation matches whether you think friction is useful or not.
a) useful – it stops you slipping.
b) useful – it stops the car skidding.
c) not useful – it stops you going fast.
d) not useful – it slows the bicycle down (or it makes it harder to pedal).

2. a) smooth – you want to slide easily on it.
b) rough – you do not want cars to skid on it.

3. Ice or snow makes the road slippery.

4. a) Carol's
b) Her dice is going along the polished part, so friction will be less and her dice will not slow down as quickly.

Pages 12 and 13

1. She must have used the same piece of wood, and dragged the trainers at the same speed.

2. a) D
b) D
c) B
d) B

3. Trainer D had the best grip, because it took the biggest force to pull it. Trainer B had the worst grip, because it took the smallest force to pull it.

4. to get more accurate results

Answers

Page 14 **1.** to give them low water resistance (**or** so they can go fast)

2. **a)** A
b) Its shape has the lower water resistance, so it will fall faster.
c) to make the test fair

Page 15 **1.** **a)** Jane
b) She makes a smaller shape because she is bending down, and she has a smooth helmet.

2. **a)** Pen
b) Her parachute is bigger so it has a bigger air resistance.

3. **a)** if the size of the parachute makes a difference to how long it takes to fall
b) Bigger parachutes take longer to fall.
c) bigger (or greater), longer

Page 16 **1.** gravity, Earth, weight, force, newtons

2. $\frac{1}{6}$ N

Page 17 **1.**

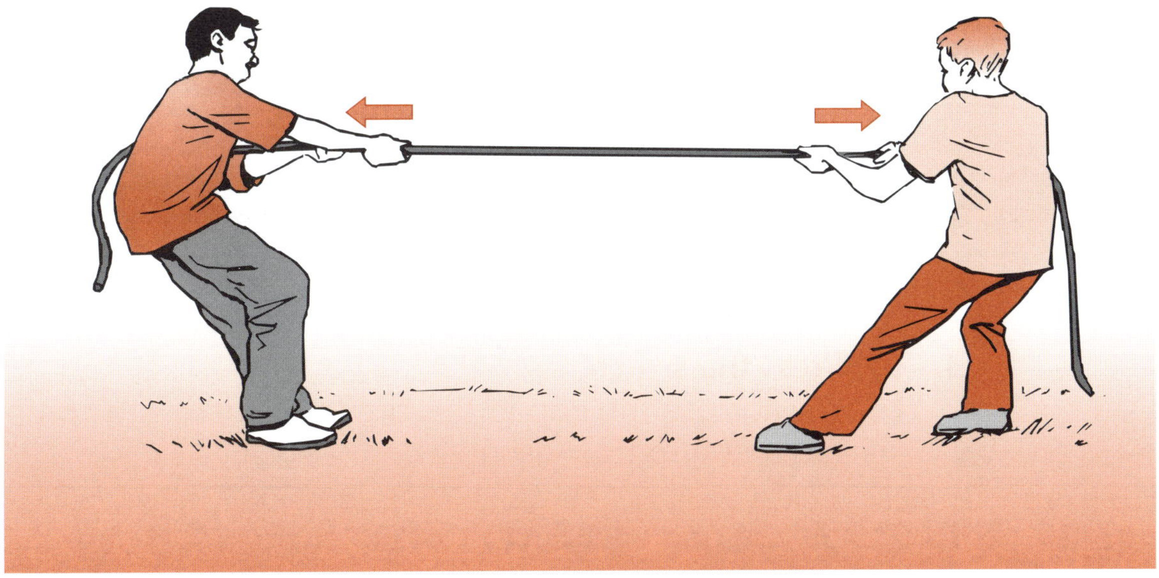

2. **a)**

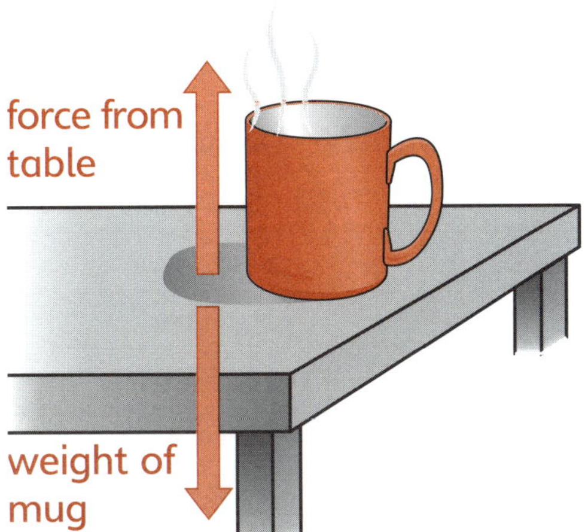

b)

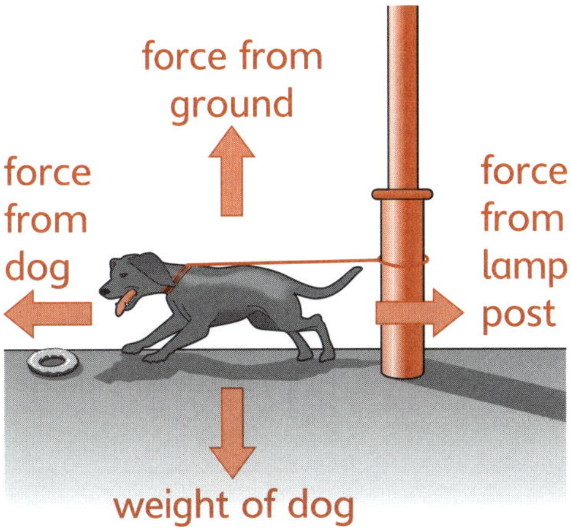

Answers

Pages 18 and 19

1. a) 150 N
b) 700 N

2. upthrust

3. a) 9 N
b) 7 N
c) 2 N
d) Upthrust is balancing some of the weight of the stone when it is in water, so the stone does not pull on the forcemeter as much.

4.

Pages 20 and 21

1. a) slow down
b) speed up

2. a) His weight is bigger than the friction force.
b) Friction is slowing him down.

Pages 22 and 23

1. a) provides electricity
b) turns when electricity flows through it
c) join parts of the circuit together

2. a) Both wires go to the same side of the battery.
b) There is no battery.
c) There is a gap in the circuit.

3. a) Press the switch.
b) It will close the gap in the circuit so there is a complete loop for the electricity to flow around.

Page 24

1. Metals are good conductors of electricity.

2. a) yes
b) The coin is made from metal, so electricity can flow through it.

3.

Material	Does the bulb light?	Conductor or insulator?
wood	✗	insulator
coin	✓	conductor
plastic ruler	✗	insulator
metal scissors	✓	conductor
drinking glass	✗	insulator

Answers

Page 25

1. They are not as powerful.

2.
- The man is about to touch a switch with wet hands.
- The kettle has a damaged wire.
- The woman is touching the pins on the plug.
- The toddler is poking something into a socket.

Pages 26 and 27

1. a)

b)

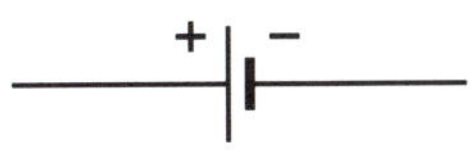

c)

2. a)

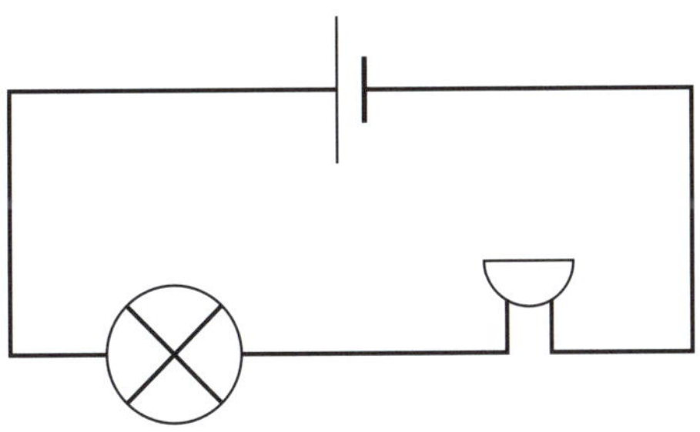

b)

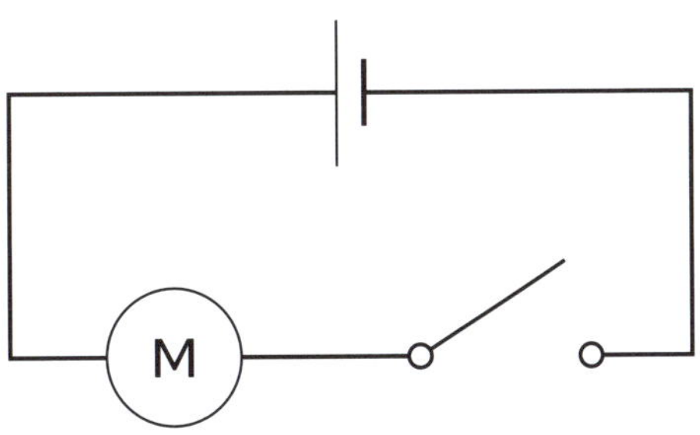

c)

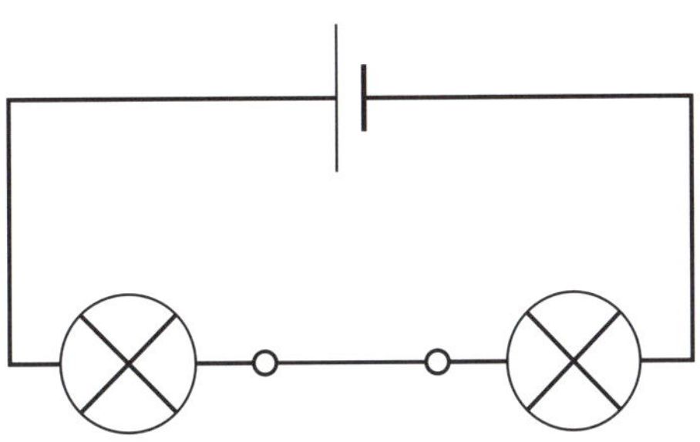

Pages 28 and 29

1. The bulb is brighter.

2. Put another cell in the circuit.

3.
- Put another bulb in the circuit.
- Take one of the cells away.

4. shortest, short, greater

5. a long, thin wire

Index and glossary

air resistance 15	**friction** caused when something moves through the air
attract 4, 5	pull towards each other
balanced forces 17, 20	**forces** that are the same size but in opposite directions
battery 22, 26	two or more cells used together
cell 25, 26, 28	part of a circuit that provides electricity (the correct scientific name for just one **battery**)
circuit diagram 26	a way of showing a circuit with **symbols** so it is easy to see how the components are joined together
component 22, 26	part of a circuit, such as a **cell**, switch or bulb
compress 8	to make something shorter or smaller by pushing it
conclusion 7, 13	what you have found out in an investigation
conductor 24	something that lets electricity flow through it
electrical circuit 22–29	a complete loop for electricity to flow around
evaluation 13	deciding how good your investigation was
fair test 6	an investigation where you only change one factor
float 18	when something stays on top of water instead of sinking
forcemeter 9, 12, 16, 19	an instrument containing a **spring** that is used to measure **forces**
forces 4–21	pushes or pulls
friction 10, 11, 12, 13, 14, 15	a force that slows down moving objects
gravity 9, 16	a force that pulls everything towards the Earth
insulator 24	something that does not let electricity flow through it
investigating 6, 12, 13	finding the answer to a scientific question
iron 4, 7	a metal that is magnetic
magnet 4, 6	something that can **attract iron**, and can attract or **repel** another magnet
magnetic material 4	a material like **iron** or steel that can be attracted by a **magnet**
mains electricity 25	powerful electricity that is supplied through sockets in the wall
newtons 9, 16	the units used for measuring force and weight
prediction 6	what you think you will find out in an investigation
repel 5	push away
safety 25	making sure you are not harmed
scale 9	the numbers on a measuring instrument
spring 8, 9	a coil of wire that can be stretched or squashed
stationary 17, 20	not moving
stretch 8	to make something longer by pulling it
symbols 26	simple pictures representing things that are difficult to draw
unbalanced forces 20	a pair of **forces** where one is bigger than the other
upthrust 18	the force from water that makes things **float**
water resistance 14	**friction** caused when objects move through water
weight 16, 18	the force of **gravity** pulling on something